SOUR

Hagakure is one of the most famous and controversial works handed down to us by Japanese literature. It contains the ancient wisdom of the samurai in the form of short aphorisms. The author, Yamamoto Tsunetomo, who lived in an era of peace and consequent decadence of the figure of the samurai, closed himself in a Buddhist monastery, where for seven years he taught the young Tashiro Tsuramoto the ancient code of honor. The student transcribed the conversations he had with the master and collected them in the eleven volumes that make up "Hagakure", a precious testimony of a complex and positive thought, very different from the stereotype of the suicide bomber devoted to canceling himself still alive

FINDING THE CALM IN THE STORM

From the wisdom of samurai sword masters the way to face difficulties and respond to change

Bereavement, adversity, illness and other painful events can strike us suddenly, wounding us deeply. The author shows us the path to free ourselves from suffering: it is the ancient way of the sword, which the samurai masters have built over the centuries with their thought and their action. A spiritual-existential path that teaches us self-discipline, perseverance and resilience, to learn to live in the present moment, always act with honor and courtesy and defeat fear. To be free in every moment of our lives.

Read the phrases you'll find by browsing the book, focus on their meaning and put their teaching into practice in everyday life. To complete the work project you are working on, to improve your relationship with other people, to gain security in the difficult moments of your life. I am sure that from each of these pearls of wisdom you will be able to draw the strength they are able to unleash.

Miyamoto Musashi

Born in the Miyamoto village in the Harima province, he was instructed in the use of weapons by his father Munisai, who was a swordsman recognized by the shōgun, while the Zen monk Takuan Soho, a friend of Yagyu Munemori, a famous sword master, also contributed to his spiritual development. At 13 he had his first duel to the death. At 16 he participated and fought in the epic battle of Sekigahara (1600) for the defeated faction, that of the daimyo of the west. Having survived the massacre of thousands of warriors and pursuit by enemies, Musashi began a wandering around Japan in search of adventure and personal affirmation. After that experience that marked him deeply, he lived several years in total hermitage in the most impervious forests, dedicating himself exclusively to refining his martial techniques. He wandered until he was 29, fighting sixty times and always winning, even when he found himself fighting against multiple opponents at the same time or against martial arts masters, such as the samurai of the Yoshioka family, famous for their sword school in Kyoto. His most famous duel was the one fought against Kojirō Sasaki, known as Ganryu, in 1612, on the island of Funa-jima.

The duel had so much renown that this island now bears the name of Ganryū-jima. His lack of punctuality in appointments was legendary, but it should be noted that the lack of punctuality in duels was part of a precise psychological strategy that Musashi adopted (never repeating it more than once or twice with opponents who were aware of it), in order to take away the opponent's confidence and make him lose calm and concentration. In fact, in his most famous duel against Kojiro he was late to the point that an emissary of the challenged was sent to take him, who found him still sleeping. Musashi got up and ate his breakfast slowly. When Kojiro saw him arriving by boat, calm and armed only with a bokken, he lost his temper to the point of running towards him in the water, throwing away the scabbard of his katana. Musashi addressed him telling him that in that state he had already lost. He was an innovator in psychological fighting strategy, in the study of the opponent's personality and weaknesses and in behavioral tactics to exploit them. Strategy almost unknown until then, among the samurai.

Fast as the wind, calm as a forest, aggressive as fire, and immovable as a mountain...

You have to sail the sea
unbeknownst to the sky...

What does it mean to be samurai?
Dedicate yourself body and soul to
a set of moral principles and
achieve perfection by the way of
the sword.

The samurai advances day after day: today he becomes more skilled than yesterday, tomorrow more skilled than today. The training never ends

Step out and fall seven times, get up eight times and rise again

The value of a man is revealed in the instant in which life confronts death

The sword must be more than just a weapon; It must be an answer to life's questions

I think that the essence of pure action consists in reaching the goal after having touched the abyss of failure

When the waters rise, the boat
does the same

There is a saying: "If you wish to probe a friend's heart, get sick." Anyone who behaves like a friend when everything is going well, but then turns away like a stranger in case of illness or misfortune is just a coward

Throughout his life, the samurai must never allow himself to distance himself from those to whom he is spiritually indebted

The samurai's word is stronger than metal

It is good to face difficulties in youth because those who have never suffered have not fully tempered their character. The samurai who is discouraged or gives in to the test is of no use.

The first word uttered by the samurai, under any circumstances, is extremely important. Through this he reveals all the value of him. In times of peace, as in times of destruction and chaos, great courage can be revealed by a single word: then it can be said to be the flower of the soul.

To follow the Way, the samurai must keep his attention on the present moment and not waver, not have worldly thoughts or be a slave to passions. Every moment is important and therefore you must always focus on the present moment

Uesugi Kenshin said: "I never thought about winning, I just understood that you always have to rise to the occasion, and that's what matters. It is embarrassing that a samurai is not. If we were always up to the situation, we would never feel uncomfortable."

It is good that the samurai, even when he is about to be decapitated, manages to carry out the last action without hesitation

A samurai said: "There are two kinds of pride: the inner and the outer. The samurai who does not possess both is worth nothing". Pride can be compared to a sword, the blade of which must be sharpened and sheathed

During the attack the samurai must be in the front line and during the retreat in the rear

.

The spirit with which one man is defeated is the same spirit with which ten million are defeated

In developing a strategy it is important to be able to see things that are still distant as if they were close and to have a detached view of things that are closer

Learning military tactics is useless. If the samurai doesn't close his eyes and doesn't rush at the enemy, even if he is only one step away, all the rest will be of no use

Whoever defends everyone defends himself, whoever thinks only of himself destroys himself

The miss always seems to be the best

Here are my four vows: never be inferior to anyone in the Way of the samurai; to be useful to my daimio; practice filial piety; show great compassion and act for the good of humanity

The samurai must daily cultivate his spirit and exercise his body, so that no one - among a thousand allies - can touch him. Of course, without this preparation, he will never be able to defeat an enemy

The samurai must always avoid complaining, even in everyday life. He must always be careful never to let an expression of weakness slip by. A single word said inadvertently often reveals the value of the speaker

The samurai must feel constantly animated by the thought of still being far from perfection and devote his whole life to the search for him, assiduously pursuing the true Way. By means of a similar practice it is possible to find it

The enlightened samurai is the one who prepares and foresees all the details of the action. On the contrary, the unenlightened samurai gives rise to the painful impression of floundering in a chaotic tangle in those who see him and his success derives only from luck, since he does not examine all possibilities before acting

A samurai who has waited to find himself in difficult situations to learn his way out is not enlightened. A samurai who studies the situation in advance and foreshadows every eventuality and possible solutions is wise and, when the opportunity presents itself, he is able to face it in the best way.

Observation and perception are two separate things; the eye that he observes is stronger, the eye that he perceives is weaker.

He thinks of yourself lightly and of the world deeply

Today's victory is your yesterday's ego, tomorrow's will be an inferior man's

To give advice, first of all you need to understand if the other person is willing to accept it or not

Delving into the uncharted path, endless secrets will eventually appear

When you are determined, the impossible does not exist: then you can move heaven and earth. But when man lacks courage, he cannot persuade himself of it. Moving heaven and earth effortlessly is a simple matter of concentration

A downpour imparts the teachings of him. If the rain surprises you halfway, and you walk faster to find shelter, you will still get wet when you pass under the eaves or in the open areas. If, on the other hand, you admit the possibility of getting wet right from the start, you won't be bothered, even if you get wet anyway. The same disposition of mind, by analogy, is valid on other occasions

Those who are euphoric on happy days will be depressed on sad ones

Those who boast of their abilities
by deeming themselves superior
will inevitably be punished by
Heaven

Until man rises to the top it is difficult to understand the infinite capabilities inherent in him

Learning to listen to the words of others, to read books and suspend judgment - these are the tools to achieve the judgment of the ancients

A person's dignity can be judged by the first impression he makes. There is dignity in effort and diligence, in serenity and discretion. There is dignity in observing the rules of the code and in righteousness. There is dignity even in gritting your teeth and keeping your eyes open: all these attitudes are outwardly visible. What is of importance is to always act with dignity and sincerity

Life lasts only an instant; it is necessary to have the strength to go on doing what we like best. In this world as fleeting as a dream to live in suffering, doing nothing but unpleasant things is sheer madness

Individual abilities don't change much, but with practice of training one can reach a level that is difficult to classify. If a person brags about his level, believing that he is high, that just shows how low he is

There are many in the world who are willing to teach; those who receive it with pleasure, on the other hand, few; even less, then, those who adopt the teaching received

Printed in Great Britain
by Amazon